CW01082610

Poems and Points

HARRI WEBB

Gomer Press
1983

First Impression - October 1983

ISBN 0 85088 526 4

©   Harri Webb 1983

Printed by
J. D. Lewis & Sons Ltd.
Gomer Press, Llandysul

Refresh your incke with wine or
vinegar when it waxeth thicke.

from 'The Preceptes of Writing'
  in *The Petie Schole* by Francis Clement 1587

CONTENTS

FRATERNAL GREETINGS

The people's flag's red-white-and-blue
And several other colours too.
See lining every tainted fold
A tarnished fringe of Saxon gold.

So raise the venal banner high,
For Sale! For Sale! is all our cry,
And neath its shade we'll try like hell
To sell our native land as well.

Corruption's black and envy's green
Upon the leprous folds are seen,
And guiding us through shades of night
The Yellow Streak shines broad and bright.

So hoist the harlot emblem high
Above the fragrance of our sty
Sustaining us in all our frauds
Until we reach the House of Lords.

Come clown and cretin, thug and sot,
Let's all hang on to what we've got,
Work every ruse, however vile,
Till each has made his little pile.

So raise the stinking standard high.
We stumble onwards soon to die,
A shambling shower of senile wrecks,
The Dragon's breath's hot on our necks.

COX'S FARM

My uncle kept a public house,
The Glamorgan Arms so neat,
It stood just off the Mumbles Road
At the end of Argyle Street.

And when I was a little boy
My Uncle Wil so kind
Would show me the walls of Swansea Jail,
So high and huge and blind.

That's where the wicked people go
To save us all from harm,
So watch your step in life my lad,
Don't end in Cox's Farm.

It is no rural residence
But a place of dismal fame,
No flocks they keep, no crops they reap,
Its harvest is of shame.

The gasworks stink and the buffers clink
As the shunting trucks go by
And each man stares through prison bars
At a scrap of Sandfields sky.

But the tree of liberty shall grow
From that dark and bitter earth
For patriots bold its high walls hold
In the pangs of a nation's birth.

Here's a health to all who've made a stand
To keep our land from harm
And served their spell in a prison cell
And dwelt in Cox's Farm.

BAD JOHN

John has been a naughty boy,
John is being kept in,
He disobeyed his master's voice
And that's a mortal sin.

He damaged public property,
He went against the law,
He carried on improperly
So they've given John what for.

One day they came and fetched him
And far away he's gone,
They threw the bloody book at him
And said, That's the end of John.

They put John under lock and key
And his outlook seems quite grim,
For none may write him letters
And none may visit him.

I wonder why they're so frightened
Of 570353?
Is it because they realise
That John's the one who's free?

THE NOBLEST WORK OF GOD

Come all you jolly voters
And listen to my voice;
I'll tell you of a party
That now should be your choice.

And if you only trust them
Then you'll have no regrets,
For they always keep their promises
And always pay their debts.

For they are sober citizens
Who all lead moral lives,
They are honest over money
And are faithful to their wives.

They are full of all the virtues,
Let us praise them to the sky;
They are not like the others
Who cheat and steal and lie.

They're such a noble party,
From the truth they never swerve,
And if you put your trust in them
You'll get what you deserve.

FROM RISCA WITH LOVE

I'm a citizen of Mummersher,
I'm as English as the Queen,
And I ates them rotten Welshies
Wot paints the signposts green.

I've always lived in Mummersher,
Now they wants to call it Gwent,
But I can't pronounce that ard foreign word,
It do make my teeth all bent.

I ates their orrid language
Wot I can't understand,
It should be a crime to speak it,
I'd like to see it banned!

There's no room for it in Mummersher
Wot's as English as Surrey or Kent,
Though I've eard there's schools wot teaches it
And there's kids wot thinks they're in Gwent.

Just ark at em jabbering at it
Like monkeys in a zoo!
Talk English tidy we gotto, innit,
Like wot ew an me do do.

HISTORY AND PROPHECY

Oh they're coming down to Williamstown
With their faces full of worry
And, so we're told, they want miners bold
And they want them in a hurry.

They want coal again and they want the men
Who'll go down the hole and cut it,
But the miners' lads have asked their dads,
And they've told them where they can put it.

Our English friends are at their wits' ends,
For fuel they're in trouble,
For they sank their brass in North Sea gas
And that was North Sea Bubble.

And the lands of oil are on the boil
And the tankers have stopped sailing,
And the stupid swines who closed the mines
Are wringing their hands and wailing.

From underground there come no sound
In seams that have been forgotten,
And the pithead gear looms gaunt and drear
Over towns that were left to go rotten.

And there's many a louse up in Hobart House
Who's wishing that he'd heeded
The men who said, Before you are dead
The pits are going to be needed.

But they treated with scorn the best men born,
No land ever bred men finer,
So serve them right in their sorry plight
For doing the dirt on the miner.

HIGH RISE BLUES

We live in a tower
Just like a king
But it's really not quite
The same sort of thing
We are up here
And the ground's down there
And all around us
Is empty air.

The Tower of Babel
Was levelled flat
If we were able
We'd do that
But times have changed
And the Planning Board
Say they know better
Than the good Lord.

So we live in a tower
A vertical slum
You can see for miles
To kingdom come.
They tell us it's nicer
Than living below
And they are the experts
They should know.

But one fine day
They'll change their mind
Say, This is all wrong
We must have been blind
They'll take them all down
And recover the cost.
They can't lose
But we are lost.

MALENTENTE

I say, aren't these Frenchmen awful,
They've had an H-Bomb test
Although we said they shouldn't,
And we always know the best.

Our English bomb is different,
As they'll tell you anywhere,
It's sporting and it's decent,
And above all, it's *fair*.

It has all the English qualities
The whole world loves the most,
But we English are so modest,
We English never boast.

The Frenchmen's bomb is horrid,
One hears such dreadful tales,
They say it smells of garlic
And is full of frogs and snails.

But our English bomb is different,
You *do* see what we mean,
It's morally superior
And just like us, it's clean.

A BALLAD OF EAST MOORS

They celebrated May Day this year
By closing the steelworks down,
They said: This is the final pay day, old dear,
So now will you kindly leave town.

There are no more coal trucks shunting,
No more ships unloading ore,
So goodbye, good luck, good hunting,
You're not needed here any more.

There are plenty of other things you can do,
And you've got your money in hand,
So here's your chance to try something new,
Though there aren't many jobs in the land.

The tall chimneys looked most impressive
As they rose against the sky,
But we've got to be progressive,
So it's furnace and forge, goodbye.

We know that you've been brought up with steel,
We know it's a job for men,
We understand how you must feel
When you're offered work pushing a pen.

But you've got a government you can trust,
So don't be a nuisance, old chap,
For firms can go bust and steel can rust
And finishes up as scrap.

SEASIDE RITUAL

Season of mists and party conferences
At off-peak rates in moribund resorts,
The leaders thrill us with uplifting thoughts,
The other parties are mere pestilences,
Their empty promises are all pretences,
Agents present encouraging reports,
Delegates exchange inspired retorts,
Factions do deals, take soundings, mend their fences.

Frail words are flying like the withered leaves
That drift in the deserted public park
Where the first wind of coming winter grieves
As days draw in and early falls the dark.
Reporters write them down in little books,
The anglers on the pier bait their hooks.

FFANFFARE

A ffervent ffanatic called Ffred
And the ffierce fflock of ffellows he's led
   In their ffearless ffight
   Ffor ffreedom and right
Are the ffinest ffolk Fflint ever bred.

HOLM RULE

All hail the island Utopia
You can see from Penarth Pier,
Flat as its name, uncontoured,
No history, nothing untoward
Has ever happened on it,
It could be another planet.
Off-shore, off all the routes
Plied by the pleasure boats,
Fragment of St. Mary's parish,
Cardiff, but no garish
Flare from Tiger Bay
Ever shone this way.
Ideal republic, democracy
And dictatorship here may agree.
Only one person lives there, it's said,
And he's dead.

THE ART OF THE POSSIBLE

Let's do our best for the ancient tongue,
Its music's so delightful,
We dearly love to hear it sung,
But speak it? Oh, how frightful!

ON THE TOWN

Two farmers' boys, as you must know,
Went from Wales to the Smithfield Show.
When all the fatstock they'd admired,
As evening came they felt quite tired
And having no taste for dissipation
At a cinema sought relaxation.
Wil kicked off his shoes to ease his feet,
They slid quietly under another seat,
The air was warm, the stalls were cosy,
The film was dull and the boys felt dozy,
But that was followed by another
And now begins our spot of bother:
A travelogue by the Tourist Board
Displaying our land to friends abroad,
Playing the harp and making hay
And all the things we do every day.
The clattering clogs of a lively dance
Aroused our heroes from their trance,
Jac cried to Wil in excited tone,
Rwy'n nabod hon, dyna Winnie Jones!
Unfortunately quite forgetting
They weren't at home, it was most upsetting.
The language of heaven fell strange on the ears
Of the audience there, it aroused their fears,
Wil groped for his shoes he couldn't find,
They'd rolled away to a seat behind,
Further chaos, a panic wail:
They've got a bomb!

                    To abridge my tale,
The lights went on, the police appeared
(The film was ruined, it must be feared)

Our lads were seized and interrogated
Explained their plight and all fears were sated.
The policeman by luck was from Clydach Vale
And, sympathising with their tale,
Advised, For a quiet place to go
On an evening out, why not try Soho?

GRAND SLAM

The skill of the Welsh at the handling game
Is known in many lands,
And every girl will tell you the same,
It's because they've such active hands.

ANSWER FROM LIMBO

Where will you spend eternity?
The posters question us.
The answer comes quite readily:
Waiting for a Cardiff bus!

THE FESTIVAL
(Respectfully dedicated to the Mid-North-West
Wales Regional Arts Association)

Nothing much had happened there since the squire's
                                    grandfather
Had been hammered on the Stock Exchange. The
                                    church, though,
Was old, and dedicated to a Celtic Saint of whom
Nothing certain is known, but who performed
Several unlikely miracles, which were no doubt
An inspiration to the Reverend Gehazi Goat,
Archdeacon of the Antarctic for eighty years
And now put out to grass. But Ceridwen's kettle
Boiled over in his brain and within a fortnight
He'd organised a Festival. Signor Segaiolo
Was invited from Italy to play the organ, but got lost
Somewhere in Swansea, so Mrs. Davies the Drains
Grappled with Scarlatti instead; the bass coupler
                                    wasn't up to it,
But she coped, except for the twiddly bits.
There were readings by Antarctic poets, full of long
                                    silences
And blank spaces, conveying the appropriate
                                    atmosphere
Of that distant clime, and there were lecturers
From the Institute of Antarctic Literature, to explain
The depths, the subtleties, the silences,
But Plas Ucha's sheepdog ate their pet penguin.
There were paintings, too, hung on churns,
Ricks, siloes, the phone booth and the Council's JCB,
And a piece of abstract sculpture, but that got taken,
By mistake, so they said, by the gipsies on the
                                    common.

22

People came from as far afield as Llanelli
In buses that jammed the lanes just at milking time,
And the landlord of the Red Lion refused to serve
The Royal Falkland Islands Ballet Company.
What of the future? What is Art? What is life? What's
                                        the damage?
Said a spokesman, we've come through swine fever,
Foot-and-mouth, fowl pest and the last price review,
I reckon we can put up with this caper.

GRANDSTAND VIEW

Damned beyond redeeming
In the flames of Hell
Hear the sinners screaming,
Hear the tortured yell.

In the arms of Jesus,
Saved by his great love,
How their torment pleases
As I watch them from above.

CHAIR POEM

To be inscribed on the reverse of the truly inspirational poster published by The Welsh Arts Council.

Behold the Bard, throned in his chair,
His lofty brow, his tidy hair,
The strong but sensitive expression
That bears no trace of late-night session,
Clear eyes that speak a noble mind,
The rugged features, stern but kind,
The manly bearing, calm and proud
That claims the homage of the crowd,
The sort of role that could be pressed on
Some handsome guy like Charlton Heston,
Epitome of virile grace
And model to the human race.
I bow, this side idolatry—
But then a thought occurs to me:
This godlike creature on his throne
Is not like any bard I've known,
And when I turn my mind to those
My verse all but congeals to prose.
Your actual bards who rhyme and scan
Are quite a different type of man,
And not the sort you'd introduce
To any bird who wasn't loose.
They're far too partial to their grog,
Spend half the day locked in the bog,
Hypochondriac, dissolute,
Devious, debauched, of low repute,
Ungrateful, morbid and morose,
Most of the time half comatose,
Unsatisfactory, harum-scarum,
No wonder people cannot bear 'em,

And far prefer to contemplate
An ikon or a fashion-plate,
And, gazing at the beau ideal,
The iron jaw, the eyes of steel,
The barbered locks, the perfect teeth,
Say, That's what they're all like, underneath.
The public mind, with insight sure,
Thus certifies its poets pure.

FEET FIRST

To lesser breeds his brothers represent
The fading splendours of the British Raj;
He wears the honest Labour Party badge
And does the same among the wogs of Gwent.

HEARD IN THE HOUSE

We English always play the game,
But please don't think we're fools,
For if we find we're losing,
We simply change the rules.

TRISTES TROPIQUES

Into the blue lagoon sailed HMS Truculent,
Her guns covered, this was a courtesy call,
A leisurely cruise among the coral islands.
The crew were feasted on barbecued sucking-pig,
Mangoes, pawpaws, breadfruit, guavas and yams,
They quaffed the fermented juice of the cokernut
And awoke clear-headed. They were entertained
By dusky maidens in sinuous dances, and off-stage
                                                    as well
And the friendly natives performed their tribal ritual.
We must repay them, said the grateful sailors,
We will stage a show of our own. So they played a
                                                    football match.
The tall bronze warriors crowded to the touchline,
Marvelled at the white man's magic, passing,
                                                    shooting, dribbling,
The referee obviously a mighty witch-doctor,
And the goalkeeper protected by a powerful taboo.
They clamoured for instruction, begged the sacred
                                                    whistle
And trained diligently. They were natural athletes,
Keen-eyed, fearless, strong. They played barefoot
But could kick like mules, fast, low, accurate.
The crews of visiting ships were most impressed.
But there was one thing amiss. Competition
Was not in their culture. It was unthinkable
That one side should score more goals than the other,
And so every game was drawn. All the sailors
Marvelled at their play, their mastery of football.
A pity, they said, they've missed the point
                                                    completely.

All that co-ordination, strength, skill, control,
And they play every match for a draw. It was a waste
of time
Us teaching them the game in the first place. But there,
What can you expect from a lot of primitive savages?

PLEASE KEEP YOUR GOG ON A LEAD

The mountain of Snowdon is barren and bleak,
There are gogs at the bottom and fogs at the peak,
But it's worth the steep climb over boulders and bogs,
For at least when you're up there you can't see the
gogs.

VIEW FROM THE SUMMIT

Ninety per cent of the human race
At any time are an utter disgrace;
The other ten, we all agree,
Consist of such as you and me.

LINES WRITTEN ON A PAPER HANDKERCHIEF

Mankind is more marvellous
Than you'd suppose,
He devastates forests
To blow his nose.

27

LET THEM EAT COKE

The traveller stares in surprise
At the sulphur-shrouded scene,
He scarcely can believe his eyes,
Such sights are rarely seen.
He hastens on past dying trees
For here he finds no joy,
He'll never see such things as these
Except in Abercwmboi.

And they that dwell in that foggy hell
Will say, should he enquire,
That smokeless fuel burns quite well
In many a distant fire,
And it's quite a joke that all the smoke
That London would annoy
Is allowed to fall from the chimneys tall
On the homes of Abercwmboi.

On shops and houses, roofs and walls
There's a rain of grit so fine,
It smothers the babies in the prams
And the washing on the line,
And if cleanliness and godliness
As it says, are a close alloy,
We can only guess what goes on in the mess
That's seen in Abercwmboi.

When Moses led the Exodus
He gave the Jews a sign
Of cloud by day and flame by night,
Before them it did shine.

Now Ezra stands in Moses' place,
All life he would destroy,
He's encouraging an exodus
Away from Abercwmboi.

And when a voice of protest's heard
In the corridors of power,
The answer comes, Don't be absurd,
You are a cheeky shower,
You're only tedious Taffy trash,
You're only hoi-polloi,
We must have clean air in Berkely Square
And to hell with Abercwmboi!

BUTTIES ALL

We don't bear Churchill no malice
Nor think of his name with ire,
Every night in Blenheim Palace
He tubbed in front of the fire.
He cussed and swore something awful
Like all the colliers do,
He died of M.P.'s silicosis
And all his scars were true-blue.

THE TRUE SPIRIT

The game was fast and furious,
The final of the West Wales Cup,
And injury time was all the time,
But none of the lads gave up.

Two teams from neighbouring villages
Did battle in the mud,
They'd vanquished all who stood in their path,
Now both were out for blood.

They'd feuded for generations
To prove which was the better,
And today between the H-shaped posts
They pursued their fierce vendetta.

The roots of the ancient quarrel
Lay deep in the misty past,
Some said it went back to the General Strike,
And some, to Llewelyn the Last.

No wonder the game was a killer,
And the ref showed signs of strain,
And his whistle grew shriller and shriller,
And his words of warning were vain.

At last on the home team's goal line
A furious mellay broke out
As both sides strove for a vital point
That would settle the game beyond doubt.

Now was the crucial moment to prove
Which was the better team,
So they piled up in a heaving mountain
That you couldn't see for steam.

Some speak with awe of Vesuvius,
And some of Mount Etna's flame,
But you never saw an eruption
Like the one at the end of that game.

There they were all at it,
Forwards, threequarters, halves,
Bruises all over their bodies
And teethmarks deep in their calves.

With determination they struggled,
Urged on by excited cries,
They weren't the All Blacks by a long way,
But they all had lovely black eyes.

At last the ref blew his whistle
O'er the bodies strewn on the ground,
He pointed for a penalty—
But the ball could not be found.

The home team's captain addressed his men:
Look lads, I love you all,
You've fought and died like heroes,
But where the hell is the ball?

Then up spake a scarred old forward,
He looked like Jack the Ripper,
(He came from Neath), he spat out some teeth
And thus boldly addressed his skipper:

We play for the love of true sportsmanship,
Not for fortune nor for fame,
So never mind the flaming ball,
Let's get on with the game!

A FAR-FLUNG TALE

Evans the Empire had spent years in the East,
                                        prospecting.
Gold, oil, uranium, you name it, he'd prospected it.
His life had been spent in the far places, off the map.
Often he'd dreamt of home, the little old Welsh
                                        village
Lost in the hills, but when the time came, after many
                                        years,
For him to take his leave, he was not quite sure
He wanted to get back there in all that much of a
                                        hurry.
There were perhaps reasons for that, but these
Belong to another saga. Suffice for now to say
He decided to make the journey not by jumbo jet,
Pampered by pneumatic air hostesses, but the old way
By train, so he'd see something of the vast spaces
That lay between him and his homeland, gathering
                                        perhaps
Fresh adventures on the way, new tales to tell
When at last he thumped on the brass knocker and
                                        shouted,
Mam, where's my tea?
            He packed his gear and jumped onto his camel.
After many days he reached the railhead, a shack
                                        crouching
Near the ruins of a city sacked by Genghis Khan
And haunted by demons. He knew the station-master,
Old Abdul, wise in the immemorial wisdom
Of his ancient race. After the customary salutations
Which took some time, he came eventually to the
                                        point.
Abdul, he said, I'm going home at last.

But I want to go by train, see, so I need a ticket
From here to—Cwmtwrch. Old Abdul looked at him.
Truly Allah had deprived this one of his reason
To utter such a strange request. A hyena howled,
Vultures hovered, the pitiless sun beat down,
Boundless and bare, the lone and level sands
Stretched far away. At last old Abdul spoke,
Sahib, bwana, effendi, I am a busy man
With many responsibilities. Please make up your
                                                mind.

Upper Cwmtwrch or *Lower* Cwmtwrch?

OUR SCIENTISTS ARE WORKING ON IT

What Wales needs, and has always lacked most
Is, instead of an eastern boundary, an East Coast.

TON UP

There was a young fellow from Fleur-de-Lys
Whose motor bike was of great peur-de-lys,
    Sometimes just for fun
    He'd knock up a ton—
That's a hundred mile an heur-de-lys.

33

WIDER STILL AND WIDER
*(Translations made at the Rotterdam International
Poetry Conference)*

Original:
Two lands at last connected
Across the waters wide
And all the tolls collected
On the English side.

Traditional

Irish:
Dhá thir a ceanglaitear
Thar droim na saile
Is Léathgo inbailitear
ag Gaill gach taille

Michael o Huanachain

Breton:
Di'ou vro erfin unanet
A-uz da red an naoz
Hag ar jiriz-treuzi jaket
Nemed gand tud Bro-Zaoz.

Per-Jakez Helias

Dutch:
Verbonden zijn twee landen
Door water lang verdeeld
Het tolgold wordt in handen
Van Engeland gespeeld.

Leo Neilssen

Castillan:
Dos tierrsa al fin ligadas
Sobre las anchas aguas
Y todas las cuotas cobradas
Del lado ingles.

Homeros

French:
Enfin deux pays sont unis
Pardessus les flots bouillants
Mais le péage est recueilli
Par l'Angleterre uniquement.

Jean-Clarence Lambert

Serbo-Croat:
Prës vody dvë zemë
koneönë spojené
na Anglické stranë
všechno clo složené.

Jana Beranova

REDEVELOPMENT

Twice I have seen my native town
By wrath and greed to ruin brought down,
Once from the sky by those called Huns,
And once again by her own sons.

35

IN MY GARDEN

Thrush, you buxom prima-donna,
No wonder you're so plump and sleek,
You've done my garden the great honour
Of dining here for many a week.

Now I'm afraid your tunes don't thrill me
As they did in days of yore,
For every roundelay you trill me
I've paid in strawberries by the score.

Bullfinch, pretty ballerina,
Although your costume is so neat,
And though I wouldn't wish you leaner,
Please find somewhere else to eat.

All the sweetness I've been growing
Is music in the thrush's throat,
All the colour now is glowing
In feathers on the finch's coat.

And how my indignation waxes,
However well you play your parts,
For I, like every payer of taxes,
Begrudge a handout to the arts.

DISCRIMINATION

The cultured classes
Like the poems of *all* the Thomases
But the works of Webb
Are considered rather pleb.

ART LESSON

Van Gogh went to Britanny,
He didn't paint the fabled sea
But the common fields and the peasantry.
At Arles the ancient ruins there
To him were hardly worth a stare,
He painted the canal bridge and a cane chair.
He drank too much and cut off his ear
But I think he had the right idea.

CURED

Puffpig was smoker,
Puffpig was a lout,
Puffpig came to my house
And stank the whole place out.
I went to Puffpig's house
Filled with rightful ire,
Took things one stage further
And set the swine on fire.

THOUGHTS AT A TWMPATH

Folk dancing
Is not my sort of prancing,
I do not dig
The Bishop of Bangor's Jig.

HIRAETH FOR GLAMORGAN

In the quiet of the woodlands
Where the flowers scent the breeze
And the sweetest of the songbirds
Make their nest among the trees.
My heart is yearning for Glamorgan,
For the works, the smoke, the fire,
Where strong men in thronging thousands
Give a voice to their desire.

In exile now from what my heart loves,
With the trees, the singing bird,
The cares of men yet draw me to them,
Only by these my harp is stirred.
All my song is for Glamorgan
And the ever-restless crowd,
There's my heart and there's my music,
That's where I would sing aloud.

What are hills and what are woodlands
Where quiet rivers reach the sea?
In solitude and meditation
No enchantment lies for me.
The voices of the crowd are calling,
The murmur of the busy place,
To the men in far Glamorgan,
That's where I would turn my face.

Land of rebels, land of struggle,
Foul oppression bravely born,
Land of prophets with their faces
Turned toward the gates of dawn!

That's the place that fills my dreaming,
That's the place where I would be,
And a hiraeth for Glamorgan
Fills the very heart of me.
                    (from the Welsh of T. E. Nicholas)

A PLEA FOR TOLERANCE

Why can't people be broad-minded?
Why must they always make such a fuss?
With prejudice they're all so blinded.
Why can't everybody bc like us?

ON ENCOUNTERING A FLOCK OF SHEEP
ON ELECTION DAY

The shepherds waved their sticks and swore,
The circling sheepdogs did their chore,
The flock was jostled through the gate.
But man is master of his fate,
A consideration that consoles
As "the nation hurries to the polls".

EIFIONYDD

*(pan oedd sôn am Saeson yn codi tai haf
ar hyd Y Lôn Goed.)*

Dan greithiau hagrwch cynnydd
Er budd y blydi Sais,
Mae bro rhwng môr a mynydd
Sy'n garnedd dan ei drais,
A lle bu arad' ar y ffridd
Tai haf i sothach estron sydd.

Os am ymryson ynfyd
Y chwerw newyddfyd blin,
Dewch yma, cewch ei flasu
Ynghanol penrhyn Llŷn,
Ac ambell ffrwgwd yn y man
Rhwng llanciau Lerpwl yn Rhos-Lan.

A llonydd diflanedig
Yw llonydd Y Lôn Goed,
Mae'n ffordd ddwy-lôn ers amser
Heb le i neb ar droed.
I lan na thref nid arwain ddim
Ond ar ei hyd mae'r ceir yn chwim.

Ac wedi cyrraedd canol
Y cwmwd swnllyd hwn
A'i sgrechian diwydiannol
Cewch yma hwyl, mi wn,
Yn rhodio ffyrdd fu gynt yn gul
Gyda thwristiaid wrth y fil.

(gydag ymddiheuriad i R.W.P.)

AHA, TRAHA!

Safwn yn y bwlch! Cadwn y ffynnon rhag y baw!
Rhaid i ni i gyd fod yn barod am y dydd a ddaw!
Sylwch, maent wedi gwerthu garej ein pentre i Sais!
Gwrthdystiwn, cydwladwyr, yn erbyn y fath drais.
O ystyried shwd bobol dda sy gyda ni, mae'n all wrong
Mae fy merch i yn teacho scripture yn Southampton,
A'r mab yn rheolwr banc yn Hong Kong.

YR OND MAWR

Tai haf, mae'n warthus, ac mae rhai
Yn brwydro ac yn aberthu.
Ie, Saeson, wir, sy'n prynu'n tai—
Ond pwy sydd yn eu gwerthu?

MYFYRDOD AR FY YMWELIAD CYNTAF
Â LERPWL

O'r diwedd rwy'n deall y chwant am ddŵr Tryweryn;
I olchi lle mor brwnt 'roedd angen am bob diferyn.

A SERMON ON ST. DAVID'S DAY
(The first H-Bomb was dropped
on Bikini Atoll on March 1st
1954)

Saint David sprung his big surprise
On far Bikini's isle,
He watched the mushroom cloud arise
And allowed himself a smile.

And as that anger shook the world
He spoke to all mankind:
Heed now the warning I have hurled,
You who are deaf and blind.

God's final messenger am I,
So allow me to acquaint
You sinners with what it is to try
The patience of a saint.

To you I breathed my dying word:
Remember the little things.
Now, since quiet counsel goes unheard,
My voice in thunder rings.

And since, in all creation's scale
The atom is the least,
That is the power that shall prevail
Till all your wars have ceased.

America, I have dried your seas,
Russia, I have thawed your snows,
Europe, your ancient rivalries
Must go as a bad dream goes.

Paris, Peking and Leningrad,
London, Washington, Rome,
Are equal now with the meanest pad
That the poorest man calls home.

And for the sake of a little place,
Accounted of little worth,
Behold, I have abolished space
And shrunk the globe of earth.

Now naked every nation stands
And equal in the scales,
And those once-proud imperial lands
Are all the size of Wales.

To her I speak as a father should
As her new life now begins:
Leave whoredom, seek the highest good,
Renounce your servile sins.

Although unworthy, it may be
For this you have been spared,
To lead men's thoughts to a world that's free
Where all good things are shared.

My sign, it is the gentle dove,
So listen to my voice:
Mankind, it's time you learnt to love.
You haven't got much choice.